A
PLEDGE
FOR THE
ESTABLISHMENT
OF A
SUSTAINABLE FUTURE
(2023 and Beyond)

Author

CHRIS EMEJURU

Preface

My belief in writing the book "A Pledge for the Establishment of a Sustainable Future" was to focus on areas in which I believe were crucial in breaking the status quo, focusing on a Nation that can prosper through an honest and transparent vision. A belief that Nigeria can indeed claim this and truly become the "Giant of Africa." Outlined within the book, I detail, not necessarily where Nigeria is today, but the potential for a better tomorrow. This Pledge I fully support, however I must acknowledge one subject of concern that, like any human being, I have evolved. Within the book I proposed the Death Penalty for a criminal act which today I 100% oppose. Today, I believe in rehabilitation and that no matter how harsh the crime, the individual's life should be spared. Assumptions and biases are what I was guilty of in the past, so after much reflection, I have come to the realization that a person that commits a criminal act should not be defined by that behavior let alone be sentenced to death. That is my thinking and I hope after you finish the book from beginning to end, you at least appreciate the hope, meaning, and many more realizations of what I believe for a people, a society, and a country.

INTRODUCTION

October 2015 was my first venture into Nigerian politics. Although I did not work for the Federal Government, I was a representative of sorts. Meetings with Youth coordinators, National Secretaries, and Party Chairman, informal Press Conferences, written articles in Major publications, and Radio Interviews was not in vain but the beginning of a worldview of where I saw Nigeria, Africa, and a shaping of world powers aligned, focused on achievement. Although Democracy was (and still is) flimsy, change on May 29th, 2015 came with a new outlook on how potential could bring Nigeria to the forefront. Reality however proved, like much of Africa, that luck and an inevitable push by stakeholders both International and Domestic, created slow sparks of a movement which would be gradual at its best. At the International Young Leaders Assembly held at the United Nations Headquarters in New York, I represented the struggles of the Youth speaking on Poverty, Healthcare, and Insecurity. Gradually more youths were allowed to engage more politically which was an achievement in itself. However, these issues would still run rampant, with the International community collaborating with Nigeria (Africa) whispering the age old saying, "Help those who help themselves."

In June 2017, the countless news reports, unrelenting consumption of legislation passed into law, and people on ground convinced myself not only in becoming a Presidential Aspirant but gave me a new confidence in a view of the world and where I saw Nigeria's place in it. My foundation, the United States of America, allowed me insight into pressing issues of huge significance geared towards the elections like restructuring the country, the establishment of health care for all, payment of salaries and pensions, transparency, more woman engagement, and youth empowerment amongst others. Issues I will be elaborating more in this pledge, issues of where I see Nigeria (as well as Africa) moving towards.

For the past 20 years, my travels to Nigeria have achieved many purposes. Whether it was tapping into the vast potential of market prospects for business, visiting hospitals and orphanages, or exploring activities of recreational relief that every youth grapples with. To be honest, my venture into politics was purely accidental. I didn't choose this course but I believe it was chosen for me. I knew I wanted to make a difference and help the cause, and public service was the only answer. Everything I have embarked upon, endured, and suffered was solely to advance the vision of a stronger, united, and formidable Republic. So here were are. A vision written in manuscript of a place where I see Nigeria as well as Africa heading. I hope that your reflection after reading is the same as the inspiration I felt writing this and that is of urgency, action, hope, and expectation.

TABLE OF CONTENTS

DECLARATION

OF
A
STATE OF EMERGENCY

Given the urgency in Nigeria and practical nature of the situation, a state of emergency should be given in declaration to:

The POWER SECTOR

The HEALTH SECTOR

The EDUCATION SECTOR

The LABOUR SECTOR

The ENVIRONMENT

The ENERGY SECTOR

The AGRICULTURAL SECTOR

Insecurity (Radical Insurgent groups-Terrorism)/(Domestic Criminal Activity)/(other treason related offenses)

THE POWER SECTOR

Key Areas to be addressed:

Qualification-Participation-Transparency-Enforced Legislation

Qualification

One of the major consequences in not fully vetting a serious contender in any significant role, especially the Power Sector, is failed results. When the qualification process is not taken seriously, the results will vary. In the NERC Licensing application, space is given to Managerial and Technical expertise. This is extremely significant. However, without full unbiased implementation of this process, it is nothing more than words on a sheet of paper. Only real vetting can get real results.

Participation

It is not always the size of the capital that one brings to the table, but the personal interest vested. The guarantee of a loan or bond by an investor is not always clear, especially in cloudy circumstances. A thorough risk assessment is extremely necessary in this situation. A more pragmatic approach to real results is what I would call personal participation. Very simply, I propose that due to the situation we are in, a substantial amount of personal equity should be adjusted in relation to a bond or loan brought by an investor. And no potential licensee should be acknowledged who brings a substantial amount of debt to the table. This will ensure the investor is more aware of his/her project.

Transparency

The two proposed mentions above CANNOT be fully realized without the full arm of transparency. To create a proper, respected, initiation of checks and balances, ICT (Information Communication Technology) is the way forward. By making sure every item is checked and every process is delivered, there is no other way, especially in the 21st century, then the use of Information Technology.

Enforced Legislation

If Legislation (any legislation) isn't properly adhered to, and more significantly, if there is no enforcement, then Democracy cannot be truly recognized. The rule of law is the rule of law and NO ONE is an exception to it.

Off Grid considerations

The use of fossil fuels (Coal, etc) in generating power in this sector is becoming antiquated at its best. Using Clean Energy (alternatives to fossil fuel) would provide a cheaper alternative to the consumer, bring efficiency, and be socially responsible as well. There is room for growth in this industry as the trend is moving towards this direction.

Due to implications involving the Corona Virus, Renewable Energy seems to be the way Forward. The highly inefficient and sometimes non-dependable forms of Traditional Energy have put into consideration the need to address real issues such as: Independence, Health, and the well being of Planet Earth.

THE HEALTH SECTOR

Health, an extremely vital and significant area for development, growth, and prosperity, for Country, and for humanity, has been poorly neglected and dismissed as an area in which leadership over the years has valued less than important. It is unfathomable and unbelievable to think that government officials at the highest level don't understand the economic, social, political, and even personal repercussions this could have to a nation and its people. Diseases such as Malaria are common but better managed due to drug availability (as well as preventive measures) and even the Ebola outbreak was handled appropriately (although due to international cooperation). However, overwhelmingly much progress needs to be made in Nigeria. Lack of hospitals is not the only concern but the level of care and service provided needs improvement. Efficiency in institutions to train medical personnel to achieve their best, the placement of these students in Health Centers (Hospitals, etc), and the willingness of professionals to treat patients out of empathy and concern for well being is achievable if the right structures are put in place. Structure is key and one area is financing Health.

For too long, there have been patients admitted to hospitals only to be neglected treatment because they don't have the money to pay. Even in emergency situations. To decrease this trend, Health Insurance needs to be addressed. By having individuals pay Health Insurance companies, a reasonable amount weekly, monthly, or annually, they will be in a better position to receive treatment at Hospitals, Pharmacy's, etc. The ability of Health Insurance companies to pay these health providers can be addressed by thorough assessments and due diligence of Regulatory agencies involved.

Another structural concern is the rampant distribution of counterfeit drugs. Proper regulations and investigations need to take place to make sure the Nigerian people are protected. We are on the path forward but the right leadership is consequential to fulfilling a destiny of access to good health for all, and that includes building strong institutions, making health affordable, and eliminating illegal drug practices.

The Corona Virus has had a huge impact on our Health System. From the relegation of imports to the borders, to lack of Hospital care, Logistical failures, and minimal infrastructure for potential Health Pandemics, it has created much death and despair. But it is not what happens that creates resilience but how you learn from it. There are steps that can be taken so as to make sure that we can create a Future where the past cannot repeat itself. For example, due to the halt in imports, we must encourage Manufacturing in Nigeria. This will not only create jobs (especially in the Health Sector), but will decrease our dependence on imports. More Hospitals, Labs, and clinics are needed but more importantly at Strategic Locations that benefit the Public. This requires a proper assessment of Statistics that reflects the current state of Nigeria. Identity Management needs to be at the Forefront of this aligned with Labour and Health.Logistics in providing Palliatives such as Food, Cash, Testing Supplies, has proven unsuccessful. Therefore if Nigeria is to succeed, it must incorporate Technologies (GPS, IOT's, etc) into its overall Budget. All this is necessary to maximize the Infrastructure necessary to deal with not only future Pandemics but the overall success of our Society.

EDUCATION

For any country to truly succeed, it must invest in its people. Education is such an investment that needs to be made. Lack of infrastructure, lack of qualified personnel, lack of funding, due to lack of will by respective Governments have created an environment where potential is not being fully realized. Primary, Secondary, and University level students deserve the best. They must be able to go to school knowing that they can fulfill their dreams through having attained a good education. Without this possibility, what hope is there for a people? What hope is there for a Nation? Urgently this needs to be and will addressed during my administration.

A problem for many graduates (including University level) is that they can't find a job when they finish. Usually, options include the Oil & Gas Sector, Banking, or Government but usually they are flooded with many CV's (Resumes), supply exceeding demand. Or they find a job, but not within the discipline they studied so hard to achieve. What is the way forward? In order to create jobs, you must create businesses. To create businesses, massive investments in skills training and Polytechnic institutions must be made to spur not only security in the jobs market but overall economic growth. Investing in the Youth by incentivizing programs that allow them to see beyond the status quo of standard education, with an approach to having a basic set of skills for entrepreneurial endeavors, is where I see Nigeria heading in the 21st Century.

The Corona Virus Pandemic has brought new awareness to how we view Education. Although Health is at the forefront of Distance Learning, this has created a more efficient way to Teach Students, especially Economically. Socially, there is significance in interaction among Individuals (Teacher to Student or Friendships created), but this will all be satisfied as a new approach to Learning along with engagement will be addressed.

THE LABOUR SECTOR

A great majority of Nigerian citizens live in poverty. Many don't have access to employment. Some think they are justified through the education process only to find that there are no jobs that match their qualifications. And some want to start a business but there is no access to capital. Every Nigerian citizen deserves a life of physical, mental, and spiritual fulfillment and to achieve this there must be a reduction in poverty. The Senate introduced legislation to commence an unemployment support fund. I agree and have considered setting up a Welfare department (in procession of an Emejuru administration) that would not only assist those who are financially vulnerable but provide an avenue to where they can create employment for themselves. It's a vast endeavor but a worthy one and will provide many benefits beyond implications financially. Reducing poverty brings dignity and hope to individuals who desperately need it. It can also lift a Nation to Prosperity. When people work, they make money, when they make money, they spend. Spending helps growth overall, building businesses, creating jobs, and putting tax revenues on government books to enable it to function on behalf of the people. When people spend, society benefits. The more money spent, the better. A thorough examination of Minimum wage desire and calculation needs to be carefully analyzed.

ECONOMIC PACKAGE

(IN RESPONSE TO THE CORONA VIRUS PANDEMIC)

Nigerian Population (Est): 210,000,000

Current Unemployment rate: 23%

Percentage of Nigerians living below Poverty: 69%

The Unemployment Support Fund was introduced in the Senate in 2019. To reinforce this fund during the Corona Virus Pandemic , I proposed for the next several months a payment of 18,000 naira (Former Minimum wage) for the 69% of those living in Poverty (Which would include most who are unemployed). The estimated Price would be at most 5 trillion naira or ($14,000,000,000). I then propose, when the Corona Virus Pandemic subsides an additional 10,000 naira every month for the next 1 year to every Nigerian citizen living below poverty along with the Option of each citizen to start their own business in which the Government can subsidize Polytechnical Institutions (Technical Institutions). For citizens (Living below Poverty), who do not wish to start a business, they can continue to receive funds but at a reduced amount.

How do we pay for this?

The Federal Government recently introduced a proposal to the National Assembly of request to borrow 23 billion dollars (before the Corona Virus Pandemic) so the ambition to make Nigeria a better Nation is there. The Government can borrow from Multi-lateral Agencies (There is a Trillion dollar Cap on what they can Lend), Borrow Bilaterally, and/ or take out Money from the Nigerian Sovereign Wealth Fund. Finally, due to the cyclical and single dependence on Crude oil, I believe the time for Diversification is now. I Propose we Diversify into 3 Major areas which can create Revenue Generation: Financial Technology (FinTech)- A total volume of 800,201,498 transactions valued at 42.76 trillion naira was recorded in 2019-, Solid Minerals, and Agriculture. Through Proper Regulation and Procedure, we can exploit each of these areas for the benefit of the Nation.

What are the Benefits?

Many Nigerians are not registered in the National Database because they simply aren't Identified. Usually many are those below the Poverty Line. By providing an incentive of paying a Stipend, they can reach Institutions which are necessary in attaining their Identity (Name, Address, Contact Information, etc) as well as other information. This is significant for many reasons in which the NIMC (Nigerian Identity Management Commission), NCB (National Census Bureau), and NPC (National Population Commission) along with other relevant Agencies can prioritize. This will give us Data which can further enhance the NBS. For example, How many Males and Females are there in a specific Zone? Is he or she Married? How many Children? Where do they live within that Zone? Which Local Government Area? Which State?, etc. This will give us information which can further enhance are Economic Prospects. For example, by receiving the data, we can know where to Build Hospitals, Schools, and Roads. This Data could also provide for Businesses who want to know who their customers are and where they live, etc thereby expanding their base and maximizing their profits. THIS DATA WOULD REVOLUTIONIZE NIGERIA'S ECONOMIC AND SOCIAL STANDING and

give it Legitimacy.

THE ENVIRONMENT

To view the significance of our environment, we should look through the lens of value: Health and Economics. Carbon Emissions from fossil fuels over decades has plagued our country as well as the African Continent. Steadily, we have seen an increase in droughts, famines, and floods, a trend where if there is no intervention, our generation and future generations will suffer the consequences. Many examples and much evidence seem to support the argument that Climate Change has affected our World, and way of life. Within the Sahel Region, millions of people over many decades have depended on Lake Chad as a source of livelihood. According to research confirmed by the United Nations, over 90% of this lake has been dried due in large part to Climate Change. Recent flooding in Southern Africa, famines in many parts of Africa including Central Africa, seem to conclude that if we don't move forward, things will progressively get worse. Many Institutions, both governmental and non-governmental, are now coming to the conclusion that Renewable Energy is the future. Not only is it a rational choice in terms of life, but it makes economic sense as well.

The Oil & Gas industry has long been a significant contributor in terms of transportation, in terms of GDP, and bringing progress to many people and many nations. However, the Pendulum is shifting. We are shifting to something cleaner, something that both business and the consumer can truly benefit from. Something where the Corona Virus Pandemic has made very clear in terms of our Environment and way of life. That is Renewable Energy.

THE ENERGY SECTOR

Oil & Gas in Nigeria have long been synonymous with each other, showcasing its will throughout the World as an economic engine, both reliant on one another for both good and bad. Crude oil (and its byproducts) have created a lot of wealth in Nigeria, primarily driving the economy as the main source of revenue for all major sectors. Without this resource, there would be no advancement in the most populous nation on the African Continent. However, there are major flaws in our reliance to Oil & Gas that should be addressed. It is cyclical in nature and the price can increase or decrease at any given time. Relying on one natural resource to determine the overall impact of an economy is not wise. Therefore, a serious look at diversification should be addressed. I propose different benchmarks aside from crude oil to be addressed in the National Budget. Specifically, Financial Technology (Fintech), Agriculture, and Solid Minerals should be looked at as alternatives to the ever increasing risk of value that petroleum brings and its lessening impact on the future of energy.

Another flaw in reliance to fossil fuels is the environmental impact. For example, when pollutants are discarded, the effects on a human being can be tremendous. Waste put in our waterways, lakes, and rivers can lead to detrimental effects on what many eat and consume. So, Agriculturally speaking, more can be done with more awareness as well as proper procedures put in place.

THE AGRICULTURAL SECTOR

The Corona Virus has affected the way we produce, store, and distribute food throughout our great country Nigeria. Much has been wasted and many in this sector have been affected through business shutdown, lack of jobs, and therefore lack of opportunity. However, these problems can be solved as we look toward a new beginning. This is what I proposed during the Corona Virus Pandemic and the as the way forward:

<u>FOOD INDUSTRY</u>

According to the NBS, it list the National Average of Food Prices as followed:

1 dozen Eggs: 450 naira (est)

1Kg of Beans: 276 naira (est)

1Kg of Beef: 1035 naira (est)

1 Loaf of Bread: 303 naira (est)

1Kg of Rice: 405 naira (est)

1Kg of Chicken: 685 naira (est)

1 Unit of Milk (evaporated): 150 naira (est)

1Kg of Garri: 160 naira (est)

1Kg of Fish: 1022 naira (est)

1Kg of Yam: 190 naira (est)

1Kg of Tomatoes: 240 naira (est)

1Kg of Plantain: 207 naira (est)

The Average price per litre of Kerosene was 324 naira while the price per gallon was 1,224 naira. Although Kerosene is significant, Alternatives to Kerosene like Briquettes are cleaner, safer for the environment, and generally tend to be cheaper when cooking food.

During this Pandemic and at the Recovery stage, the Federal Government can reduce the tax burden (in the short term) of those in the Agric Sector so that prices of goods will reduce and Nigerian citizens (especially those living below poverty) can afford them.

According to the NBS, the Formal Restaurant Industry generated an estimated 100,000,000 naira (2012). To keep the industry intact I propose an immediate halt to the CIT (Company Income Tax) as well as the VAT (Value Added Tax) and provide incentives to keep and retain employees.

According to the NBS, 8 million naira was spent on the Cost of Fuel as opposed to 1 million naira which other restaurants used as a Renewable Energy source. Statistics prove that Renewable energy is remarkably cleaner, and more efficient than traditional energy and should be taken seriously by the Government.

The Informal Food Sector creates an estimated 675 million dollars a year in Sales. During this Pandemic, it is essential they remain open for business, with sensitization important in protecting themselves as well as others.

INSECURITY (RADICAL INSURGENT GROUPS)-TERRORISM

Terrorism remains the biggest threat to our National Security, Region, African Continent, and the World at large. This hate filled belief, does not create but destroy. It destroys the mind, the body, and the soul of those who participate, and those it encounters. Fueled by hateful ideology, this threat has sown the seeds of discourse, politically, economically, and socially. Three areas where a nation and people cannot survive without! Politically, funds used to combat such a threat if taken seriously and truly engaged, can be diminished with more funds being used elsewhere. A limited (non-existent) threat would provide stability, boost an economy through the likes of education and entrepreneurship, and attract much needed Foreign Direct Investment which would revitalize a Nation and Continent. Socially, there would be no need for individuals to leave their homes in terms of terror thus displacement. Communities would be able to exist in relative peace and harmony without the threat of instability. I believe prevention in line with deterrence will eventually lead to the elimination of terrorism in a large scale, but all stakeholders need to get involved including Government, private organizations, and so forth.

DOMESTIC THREATS

MILITANCY

The consistency of violence and disruption by Militants in the Niger Delta Region is part of a larger problem created by failed leadership from previous governments at the State and Federal Level. Disenfranchised youths who feel neglected by their country due to bad policy implementation, want a way out of their frustration, in which engaging in criminal activity is a way their voice can be heard. Some resolutions have been created (the Amnesty Initiative) to solve the problem, but much more needs to be done to ensure that poverty is lifted, and lawful dreams and ambitions are fulfilled. Education is critical. Officials at the Local, State, and Federal Level can do more to ensure this happens. And security is significant however it cannot be emphasized enough that Violence is NOT the answer. The answer is Dialogue. When both inhabitants and relevant authorities discuss how to resolve differences, we all move forward.

HERDSMAN/FARMER RESOLUTION

The Land Use Act varies in accordance with Northern states and Southern states. Some state governments currently allocate land reserved for Herdsman while others allocate nothing at all stating it's a private matter. The Federal Government can implement laws however it should take into consideration the origins of the crisis, how to respond, and ways to prevent it from repeating itself.

KIDNAPPING

Kidnapping is a major threat to our National Security. The effects of this despicable crime is hindering our economy (crippling FDI), Tourism, and our way of life. Political kidnappings create Government instability while kidnappings for purposes of monetization destroy a Nations character. Kidnapping drains resources and disrupts lives. It is so prevalent that it is something that amongst other issues needs to be addressed immediately. I see no other option than to propose the Death Penalty for this act as the abduction of an individual or group for political, economic, and other purposes with harmful, disruptive intent.

THE
CREATION
PLAN
AND ESTABLISHED

MINISTRIES/DEPARTMENTS AGENCIES

MINISTRY OF HEALTH

Expand Health Insurance to the Public

The Elimination of Counterfeit Drugs

Increase Qualified Medical Professionals

Improvements and Expansion of Health Care facilities

Consistency in payment of Salaries

The implementation of preventative care initiatives throughout the country.

Improvements in ICT Development to increase Transparency

MINISTRY OF EDUCATION

Increase in Infrastructure and Development of Educational Institutions

Consistent payment of Salaries/Pensions to Teachers and Professors

Increase in Qualified Professionals (Primary, Secondary, University Level)

Increase and promotion of Polytechnics/Skills Training

Increase in Scholarships

Increase in Funding of Schools (TETFUND)

Improvements in ICT Development to Increase Transparency

MINISTRY OF FOREIGN AFFAIRS

Provide Foreign Assistance (Military, Economic, etc) to countries whose vision aligns with ours.

Distribute Aid to Nations who need it out of goodwill and solidarity.

Refocus Diplomacy (Assess structure and management of Embassy's)

Improvements in ICT Development to increase Transparency

MINISTRY OF TOURISM

Increase Foreign Direct Investment

Maintain Historical Landmarks and Preservations

Boost Tourism

Improvements in ICT Development to increase Transparency

MINISTRY OF SCIENCE & TECHNOLOGY

Encouragement of Innovation through STEM

Initiation of Technology into Job training and Placement

Commence the creation of Labs and Research facilities in Learning Institutions

Improvements in ICT Development to increase Transparency

MINISTRY OF DEFENSE

More training in Ethics and Combat

Advanced equipment (Uniforms, Weapons, Vehicles,etc) for Military to handle threats.

Consistent payment of Salaries

Consistent payment of Pensions to those who have served and retired from active duty.

Improvements in ICT Development to increase Transparency

MINISTRY OF PETROLEUM

Creation of a less opaque atmosphere

Stronger laws and Infrastructure development to encourage Foreign direct investment (IOC's)

Local Content Policy

Improvements in ICT Development to increase Transparency

creation of a **MINISTRY FOR RENEWABLE ENERGY**

Creation of departments/agencies focused on Clean Energy

Improvements in ICT Development to increase Transparency

MINISTRY OF LABOR

Improved working conditions

Assessment of Minimum Wage calculations

Increased Dialogue with Unions

Improvements in ICT Development to increase Transparency

the creation of a **Welfare Department**

Those living in Poverty (Below a certain income level) will receive a Federal Allowance and possibly other benefits.

MINISTRY OF INTERIOR

A Qualified Police Force

Ethics Training & Mobilizations

Nigerian Prison Service

Prison population reduction

Better arrangements for prisoners

Proper rehabilitation services

Improved Immigration services

Improvements in ICT Development to increase Transparency

MINISTRY OF TRANSPORTATION

Proper training of Port officials in lawful conduct of goods flowing in and out of the country.

The **Nigerian Port Authority (NPA), Nigerian Maritime and Safety Administration (NIMASA),** and **Nigerian Custom Service (NCS)** should be consolidated into one functioning body.

The **Nigerian Railway Corporation Act** (as amended) should be adhered to.

Improvements in ICT Development to increase Transparency

MINISTRY OF AVIATION

Manufacturing of Equipment to reduce importations.

Payment of taxes and any other fees accruing to Debtors

Improve dramatically infrastructure at airports

Concession airports with Government support if necessary

Improvements in ICT Development to increase Transparency

MINISTRY OF AGRICULTURE

Increase in productive Family farming techniques

Advancement in production, storage, and transportation of commercial produce in a technologically driven capacity.

Improvements in ICT Development to increase Transparency

Creation of a **<u>MINISTRY on HOUSING and URBAN DEVELOPMENT</u>**

Creation of Departments/Agencys focused on Affordable Housing/Better Roads/Mass Transit,etc.

FOREIGN AID

The history of self rule for many countries on the African Continent has been shaped by disruption and instability. Civil wars, ethnic cleansing, and disease outbreaks had left many nations in need of intervention. A destiny could be reached, countries were willing to offer it, and through Government, NGO's, Private Organizations, Foreign Aid was secured. Throughout the Biafra War, during the ethnic cleansings in Rwanda, and Military coups in Zimbabwe, Foreign Assistance in Services, Press, and Finance have provided relief to countries, transitioning to a better course of governance. Without this aid, it is almost certain many countries would not have proceeded to where they are today and Developed Nations of the world deserve much of the credit. However, there is an awakening happening in Africa. Countries are seeing their worth and potential. Democracy's are strengthening. Private sectors are more robust. Human rights (although there is much work to do) is being properly assessed and valued. And the sciences are impacting a society, a Continent, and therefore the World at Large. It is fair to say that if I am to lead the Administration, Foreign Aid (from respective Governments) will not be accepted.

In order to secure a way of life for all Nigerian citizens, it is crucial that our neighbors get the resources they need. Our neighbors can be those on our borders, those on the African Continent, and even those across the seas. Terrorism and Climate Change remain a major threat to National interests and by assisting others Militarily, Socially, and Environmentally much goodwill and solidarity can be spread, thereby advancing all of humanity.

IMMIGRATION

At any point of entry, by Land, Sea, or Air, it is critical that individuals reaching Nigerian shores be met graciously and hospitably. Difficulty and harassment can no longer be accepted as Nigeria, once known as having the "Happiest" people on the planet, must continue to prove that this title is deserved. People come to Nigeria for its beautiful landscapes, its history and artifacts, to engage in official business and/or just for entertainment purposes, and as such deserve to be accommodated by its most valuable resource....its people. We are a Nation of Immigrants. Immersed in many languages, ethnicities, tribes, and cultures we co-exist in understanding that we are one people, under one flag, and that is Nigeria. In our pledge, it states, "to defend her unity and uphold her honor and glory, So Help me God." So we find strength in our diversity and have and will defend it. Currently, there are citizens from other Nations who trek long distances to come and realize the potential that Nigeria has to offer. Instability in their country, and lack of opportunity, they seek Nigeria as a place for better opportunity. Within the Immigration Act (2015), these laws allow the detention of these individuals in an environment where dignity and respect is upheld and that the proceedings are fair. They are welcome but the rule of law should not be overlooked.

Illegal activity pursues are borders at every turn. The entry and re-entry of illicit activity is destroying our character, a people, and a Nation. Border response overseen by competent patrol and heads of security need to be readily available to handle the crisis.

BUDGET ANALYSIS

(FEDERAL GOVERNMENT PROPOSAL 2018)

- According to the National Bureau of Statistics, Unemployment rate stood in double digits. To reverse this trend, more funding needs to be committed to the education sector (Polytechnics focus), Skills Training, and more emphasis on the Labor Sector to boost the economy, enable businesses, create more jobs.

- According to the Debt Management Office, as of September 2017, External Debt stood at $15.35 bn while Domestic debt stood at N12.49tn. Prioritization should be given to repaying all outside debts through diversification. Domestic debts should be paid expeditiously.

- As of September 2017, our External Reserves stood at $34.4bn. An increase allows for a proper exchange rate and a strengthened naira. However, a devalued naira is also a basis for attracting FDI and therefore a floating exchange rate system should be properly implemented.

FISCAL ANALYSIS

N8.612 TN

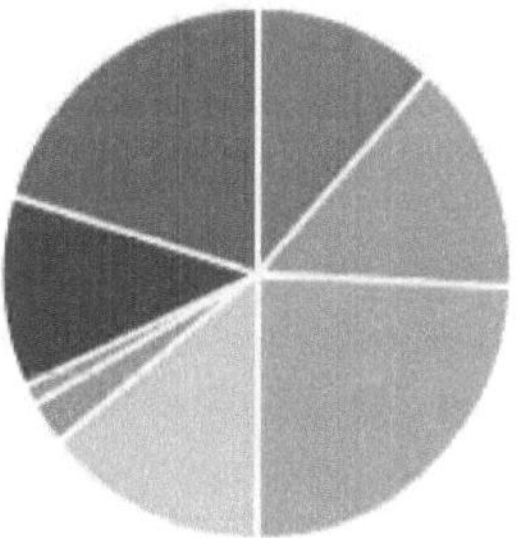

- Non-oil Revenue could substantially increase if diversification is created with emphasis on Fintech, Agriculture, and Solid Minerals
- Recurrent expenditure and Statutory Transfers can be reduced if itemized and prioritized.

These along with other appropriate critiques will increase revenue, cut costs, and therefore decrease or even eliminate the deficit.

EXPENDITURES

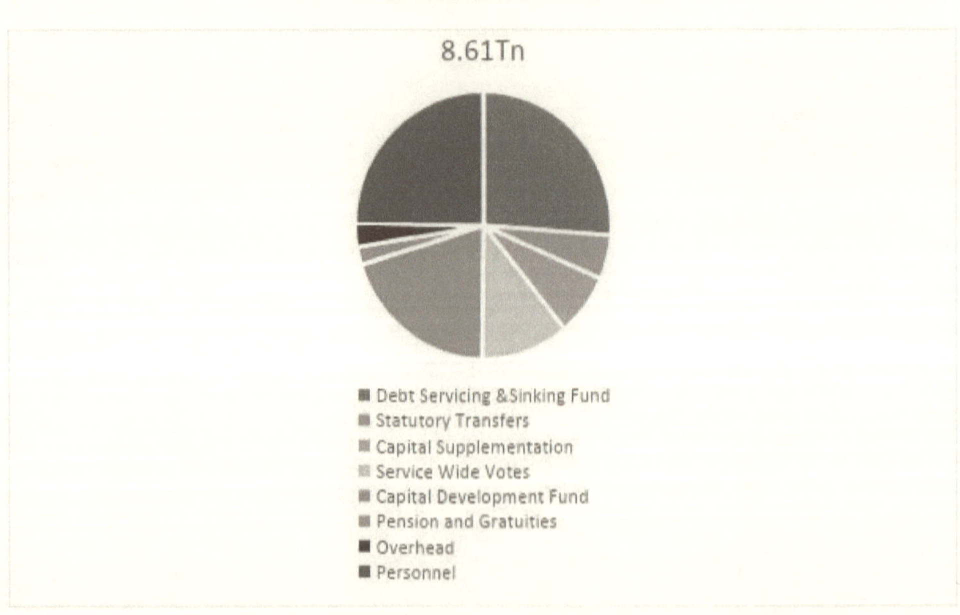

N456.4 BN

· The National Assembly consist of many constituencies forming the House and Senate. Its purpose is to serve the people of Nigeria within their districts. Aspirations to serve should not be based on financial gain but to further Nigerian interest. Therefore, there should be a cut in the budget so those who truly want to serve, do it for love of country and nothing else.

OVERHEAD/PERSONNEL

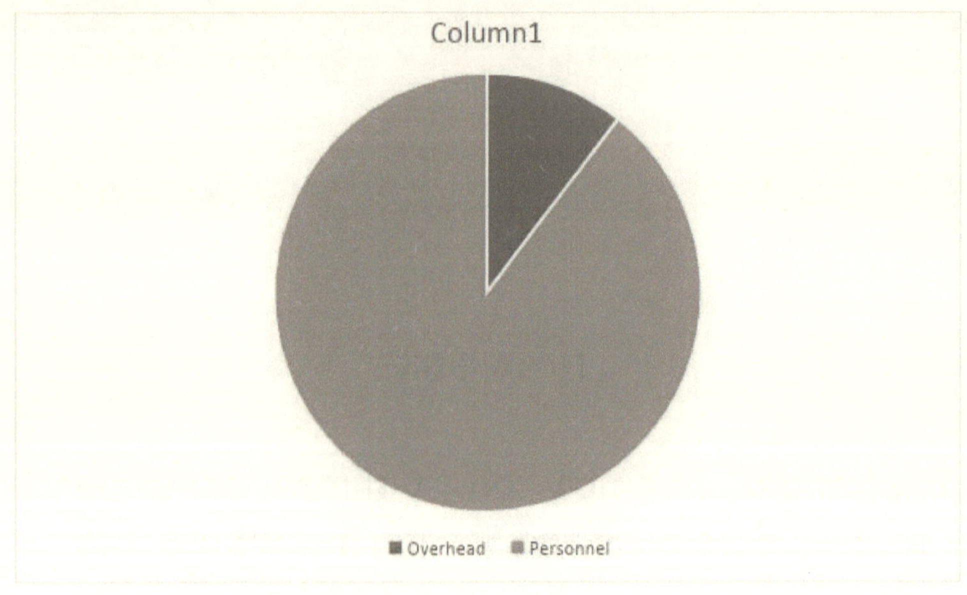

Overhead and Personnel cost can be substantially reduced if prioritized accordingly.

SERVICE WIDE VOTES

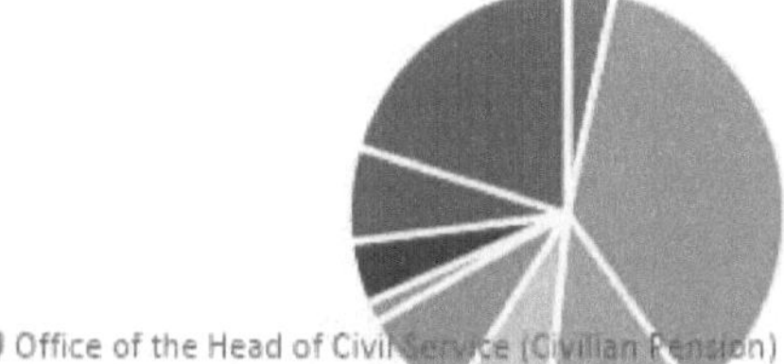

*Our Military remains the crown jewel of our Federation. It protects our Land from those who try and harm the spirit and unity of our great Nation. They sacrifice life and limb so that every citizen has the opportunity of freedom and prosperity. We must never forget them. Therefore, I propose a substantial increase in Military Pensions and Gratuities, and Equipment and Training for all Military Operations of our Armed Forces.

<u>**PRESIDENTIAL AMNESTY PROGRAM**</u>

Funding including payments of stipends should be actualized in the Presidential Amnesty Programme for re-integration of transformed Ex-militants.

<u>CAPITAL ALLOCATIONS BY MINISTRIES</u>

According to the Budget office, Power, Works, and Housing was allocated the most money with a total of N555.88bn. Defense came 4th with N145bn. Health and Education were near bottom with N71.11bn and N61.73bn respectively. In order to ensure the survival of a Nation, it is critical that there must be an increase in (amongst other areas of the budget) Defense, Health, and Education.

<u>CAPITAL SUPPLEMENTATION</u>

Within the Proposed Budget 2018, N638bn was allocated towards selected projects. More attention should be given towards Road Projects, Railway Projects, Health Projects, and Education Projects.

INFORMATION COMMUNICATION TECHNOLOGY

In order for Government to increase Transparency, create Efficiency, and gain respect nationally and internationally, ICT (or IT) remains a critical component. Securing sensitive information, improving data storage, and reduction in manual labor are just a few reasons why Information Technology is so important and needs more emphasis in Nigeria today. Many countries have met or surpassed the quota of information technology development and usage. Nigeria can continue this trend if Government works with the Private Sector not only regulating industries, but encouraging development in innovation. Increased programs and funding mechanisms can bring technologically driven Youths and entrepreneurs to their full potential, creating a competitive fire of Nigerian advancement amongst the Nations of the World. So, what is the significance of the Government and Private Sector working together? It is the People! That is the end result. To make life easier for every Nigerian citizen. A strong technologically driven Government would be more capable in the management of resources and information, thereby working effectively with the Private Sector, both functioning on behalf of their constituents. I see no other way for Nigeria to move forward, except with advancement in Information Communication Technology development.

SPACE EXPLORATION

Space Exploration. Humanities greatest quest. The unknown finally ripe for exploration due to advancements never seen before in human history. From the moon, a Flag sits, filled with hopes of more discovery from all Lands. The spark of imagination. The birth of improvement. The generous nature of its creativity. An example for Africa, ready to take the lead and fulfill its destiny within the Universe. Visionaries have chosen their path. Elon Musk chose Mars. Space programs created through Science & Technological development create a canvass for more to explore truths beyond Earth and all we know. The final frontier. The future whose work past and present should never be taken for granted. Science created it. Imagination propelled us. Vision allowed us to think beyond what is possible. And now possible is truth. Nigeria has the potential and Africa is getting ready. Our World has reached its most ambitious phase of exploration. A new beginning to chart history's misconceptions into truths waiting for us to grasp.

ABOUT

THE

AUTHOR

Chris Emejuru
A Pledge for the Establishment of a Sustainable Future (2023 and Beyond)

I was born in Alexandria, Virginia U.S.A December 1, 1982. The first of 5 children we would later relocate to Virginia Beach, Virginia where I would spend my Adolescent years. Although I was an American citizen, my Mother made sure we never lost our Nigerian (African) Identity. Whether it was preparing meals she grew up eating (Pounded Yam with Okra Soup or White Rice with Stew), or attending Traditional Gatherings of friends and family members celebrating Ikwerre (Igbo) culture, my parents made sure we never forgot the meaning of Emejuru. Growing up, I could remember stories of Hero's past, from the charismatic Leader Ojukwu, to the optimism of Gowon, the Significance of Obasanjo, and even the Apartheid Movement led by Nelson Mandela. But it was my trip back to Nigeria in 1999, which reintroduced me to hopes of a better Country, and a new beginning. There I met relatives I had never met before, a trip that gave me a new sense of Identity and purpose, and a transitioning of Power which would commence the beginning of Democratic Rule. All this would shape the beginning of a world view that intrigued my perceptions. On my way back to the States, I was more attentive in school and graduated to the University. However, it was in 2004 where I traveled to Nigeria and knew that this is where Home was. During the next 10 years, I would start businesses (some successful and some not), visit orphanages, and engage in recreational activities with family and friends, but it was in 2015, having witnessed the ups and downs in Nigeria, I decided to enter the Political Landscape. I was inspired by a new era of change. A change that would never come to be. So, it was in 2017, where I met a group of Nigerians who shared my beliefs. A belief of Youth Empowerment, Woman Development, and a better system of Governance for all Nigerians. That is when I decided I would become a Presidential Aspirant. I withdrew from the Presidential General Elections that were held in 2019 for reasons beyond my control, but that did not stop my love for Nigeria. In June 2019, I initiated the Chris Emejuru Foundation with the Goal of eliminating Poverty throughout the Six Geo-Political Zones of Nigeria through Education, Training, and Human Capacity Development. During this period, I would also write the manuscripts to the book which would eventually become "A Pledge for the Establishment of a Sustainable Future 2023 and Beyond. And in March 2020, I would create "The Advisory Force for a Stable Nigeria" (AFSN) in response to the Corona Virus Pandemic.

The purpose I had for writing this book was to share my vision of a place of not where Nigeria is now but where it can be. I wrote it not to shed light on the past, but a future written for Generations to come in Nigeria, and Africa based on a World point of view. The future starts now and together we will reach our Destination.